UNPLANNED JOURNEY:

Understanding the Itinerary

SUSAN G. MILLER, MS

Unplanned Journey: Understanding the Itinerary
Copyright © 2000 Susan G. Miller

Kaleidoscope Kare Press
110 Pheasant Run Road
Wilton, CT 06897

(203) 762-5713

A portion of the proceeds from the sale of this book
will be donated to the Alzheimer's Association.

Publisher's Cataloging-in-Publication
(Provided by Quality Books, Inc.)
Miller, Susan G.
    Unplanned journey : understanding the itinerary
/ Susan G. Miller. -- 1st ed.
    p.cm.
    ISBN: 09679584-4-X
    1.Alzheimer's disease--Poetry. I.Title
PS3563.I41995U57 2000   811.6
                      00-131133 CIP
                          QBI00-400

cover design by Mendocino Graphics

Book production by Cypress House
www.cypresshouse.com

Printed in the United States of America

To my husband, Don

Contents

Introduction

Imagine the shock of having your fifty-five year-old husband diagnosed with Alzheimer's disease and suddenly joining the four million Americans who have the disease.

Unplanned Journey: Understanding The Itinerary is the first in a trilogy of reflections about one caretaker's struggle to cope and make sense of Alzheimer's disease—a disease that society erroneously regards as a disease of the elderly.

The very nature of the word journey elicits thoughts of preparation—be it a vacation or a life passage—but an unplanned journey denotes little or no preparation and brings with it an air of uncertainty. It is the loneliness and isolation of the disease that inspired me to record my thoughts. While there are stages that both patient and caregiver pass through, the difference with Alzheimer's is that there is no itinerary to follow. One of the hallmarks of Alzheimer's is the uniqueness of the disease to each individual.

The task of caring for a family member with this chronic, incurable, neurodegenerative disease is daunting. A disease that Nancy Reagan described as "the long good-by" is characterized by gradual onset of progressive memory loss and cognitive and functional decline. The loneliness of patients' families from a lack of public understanding is one of the worst features of this disease. Currently it has been estimated that one in ten families has a member with Alzheimer's. The toll of caregiving on families is predicted to grow as nearly one out of three baby boomers, often involved in the care of elderly parents, move themselves into the age of highest risk.

The book is written as a testimonial to the wellspring of hope, understanding and compassion that is inherent in the human spirit. Much has been written on the tasks of the caregiver and the medical aspects of the disease; this book chronicles the emotional journey that caregivers—whether they be caring for parent, spouse relative or friend—travel along.

Beginning

The years or months before a definite diagnosis of Alzheimer's are often the most difficult and most frustrating for family members, who suspect something is wrong but can't quite put their finger on it. It is this insidiousness that makes the disease so difficult to pinpoint and that causes family members to question their perceptions and judgment. Most caregivers categorize this period as a time of increased frustration, turmoil, and escalated tension.

Along the way there are many signposts but, unfortunately, they most often can only be read in retrospect. Since no one wants to think that the strange and different behavior that is occurring is Alzheimer's, it's not uncommon for families to chalk it up to stress or old age. Denial is a normal and integral part of the process. However for each family there seems to be a defining moment when denial no longer works. Following the official diagnosis there is often another period of denial that allows family members a time to adjust to the reality of the diagnosis and prepare for the changes coming.

This beginning is often passed through in a haze of shock and disbelief. It is an extremely turbulent time as caregivers struggle to cope with the news and to make myriad plans for both the present and future. Ironically, it is often the details that give caregivers a respite from the shock. Caregivers struggle to understand and make sense of a disease that is so devastating and comes with no itinerary to follow. There often is a great sense of relief that, finally, there is a reason behind the loved one's increasingly strange behavior. It is a time of beginning the process of acceptance, adjustment, and planning for the future.

Beginning

We sit in the psychologist's office
the one whom my husband has been referred to upon my
   request to understand his increasingly strange behavior
behavior that myriad doctors can seem to find
no medical basis for
we sit awaiting the results of a recent battery of IQ tests
the doctor begins with small talk,
inquiring how we have been
we, or at least I, am in no mood for small talk
my husband sits with a vacant look upon his face
staring straight ahead
"It's not good, the doctor tells us, there's been a significant
   drop in IQ "
he wants us to see a neurologist
in shock and understanding combined, I blurt out,
"Our life is over"
and from some place far away I hear him say in the soft,
   controlled voice often used by psychologists,
"Your life is not over."
my husband continues to stare, unaffected by the news

I am called out of a meeting for a phone call from the
   neurologist

who dutifully calls after each and every test with results
"It is definite, as definite as it can be" he says
adding his condolences
but this time I do not blurt out our life is over
I simply thank him, hang up the phone,
and begin our new life

So Many Questions

I need passports,
aren't they required for entry into and exit from a foreign
  country?
what if they ask me how long we're staying, what shall I
  answer?
and how will I tell them only one is returning?
or do they already know?
how long will the journey be?
what places will it take us to?
is there an itinerary to follow?
or do we simply wing it?
have I packed enough?
or too much?
and what about the language?
does anyone know I don't speak it?
who signed me up for this?
why did I not have a say?
overnight I have become a reluctant traveler
not wanting to go far from home
to venture to strange places
how did I become a tour guide?
didn't anyone tell them my role has always been passenger
content to enjoy the scenery?
would they even listen?

Journey

I want to journey to the Orient, ride in a rickshaw
kayak down Baja into Mexico
hike the rain forests of Costa Rica
take the Orient Express across Europe
cruise on the QE2 to London
ski the Zermat
bike Provence, ride a barge through Holland
sit in small cafes in Rome and watch the world go by
visit Sedona and get in touch with the mystical
travel the United States in an Airstream
so much I want to do
so much we planned to do
waiting for this time in our life when it all would be possible
but now our life is defined by familiarity
routines to follow, pills to be taken
schedules adhered to
increasing dependency the theme
mealtimes, the highlight of the day
bedtime now the shining hour
I am still young, full of dreams
but well aware my time is running out
the moment is now
but overnight I've been thrust into a world devoid of dreams
this is not the journey I had planned on

Six Weeks

Six weeks
from start to diagnoses
six weeks that would forever change our life
and our concept of who we were and who we would become
six weeks of trying on various diagnoses
settling for syphilis
wishing for a brain tumor
thinking depression a real bargain
hoping all along, for something less terrible, less invasive
not as insidious
six weeks is all it took to take away hope

Thought

I thought we were immune
how naive of me
how arrogant
to think the gods would bestow upon us special
  consideration
but family genes full of longevity and good health
traced back to preceding generations
gave me no reason to think otherwise
why would our lives not be equally blessed?
and if somehow we escaped such blessed fate
Alzheimer's was never even a consideration
how naive of me
how arrogant

Kaleidoscope

I am looking at our life through a kaleidoscope,
or so it seems
nothing remains the same
everything in perpetual motion
changing with a twist and turn
an array of emotions bursts forth
in varying sizes and patterns
sometimes the brilliance is overwhelming
sometimes the sheer motion is dizzying
nothing remains the same
adapting and changing, adapting and changing
as we will do now, from this moment on

Known

I have known for a long time
months, perhaps even years
known through intuition
known through dreams
known the way a woman knows
known the way a wife knows
that something was wrong
terribly wrong
but not once did I ever know it was Alzheimer's

Retrospect

He always crossed every 't', dotted every 'i',
took his time — thorough to a fault
oblivious to the pressing needs around him
so when he began to move more slowly
increased his level of anxiety
I thought nothing of it, barely noticed
only in retrospect

he always was somewhat messy
unaware of the impact on others
leaving a trail of where he had been
so when the clutter grew
when the hoarding began
I thought nothing of it, barely noticed
only in retrospect

he always was somewhat unorganized
a caricature of the absent-minded professor
critical details left forgotten
so when he seemed to overlook things
failed to follow through
I thought nothing of it, barely noticed
only in retrospect

he always was somewhat quiet
reticent by nature

content in his world of solitude
so when he began to withdraw
become less connected to his surroundings
I thought nothing of it, barely noticed
only in retrospect

Standing Still

For the longest time I felt our life was standing still
while the rest of the world moved on without us
as if somehow, somewhere, life had come to a slow halt
I couldn't define it or explain why
but I knew it to be true
we had become like his parents
living a life of reduced options
increased isolation
safe and secure from the world
dependent on each other
every time I wanted to invite friends to Vermont,
I was met with resistance
"It's so much nicer to be alone" was the reason given
at that point I didn't understand the translation,
"I do better with just you"
nor do I think he was even aware there was a translation
he had become his father
in your face interruptions
without boundaries
my time, his time
he had become his mother
a litany of aches and pains
early to bed, late to rise
the focus of the day the next meal

he no longer worked
nor made an effort to
he was content with the status quo
and when I came home at night,
I brought the only world he seemed to need
a collection of moments and events finally made sense
the feeling our life was standing still
no longer my imagination

Defining Moment

Incidents occur, so strange they are dismissed,
only to be forgotten
or so ordinary they are taken for granted, barely noticed
not in any order, but randomly scattered
throughout the months, even years
before someone really takes notice
and then suddenly the incident
becomes the defining moment
an epiphany, the a-ha!
how were signs missed? we ask incredulously
but why might they not be missed when we use
the continuum of "too young or just a part
of the aging process" to assure ourselves
nothing is wrong?
what is it that propels us to this defining moment?
our weariness unabated?
our defenses broken down so that
the truth can no longer be hidden?
many moments comprised of collected incidents
but always one defining moment
different for every family
the car rear-ended

the way home forgotten
the blank look

and suddenly we know
as if we are seeing for the first time
what we missed all the other times

Decisions

There are many decisions to be made
so many they can be broken into categories
disease:
are we sure the diagnosis is correct?
what about a second opinion?
do we have the right doctors doing the right things?
financial:
should we sell the stock?
should we invest in bonds?
do we take an early pension?
management:
should we stay in the house he is familiar with?
should he continue to drive?
and what about skiing ?
family:
do we spend vacations with family versus the two of us?
should we move closer to family?
where should we draw the boundaries?
friends:
who should we tell now and who later?
who will we be able to count on?
will we be able to weather the losses with understanding?
many decisions to be made

most clear-cut by nature
it is the **personal** decisions that are the most difficult
do I leave my job, give up my career
to stay home and take care of him?
to enjoy the time we have left — an early retirement of sorts
a no-win situation,
the losses and gains evenly divided
regrets inherent whatever decision is made
and what of the ones that **loom** ahead
will I take care of him
or will I put him in a nursing home?
and though advanced directives are in place,
will I be able to carry through when the time comes?

Mirror

Sometimes I catch a glimpse of myself in the mirror
or become aware of my repose
and I wonder who I am
surely not the person I used to be
she is not reflected back to me
instead I see a countenance that is old beyond years
as if my spirit left one day, unnoticed

Surreal

It all seems so surreal
my husband in diapers someday
unable to communicate
not knowing anyone
the progress that this disease will take
I read about it in the literature, full of well-documented cases
the doctor speaks briefly of it in his pedantic educational
　　lecture mode
people in support groups tell tales of horror mixed in with
　　comical moments
but it doesn't seem real
surely it won't happen to us
we will be exempt
even as I see this wish for what it is
even as I acknowledge my denial
I think it will be different

The Mind

Look close
no, push it away
I am caught in a game of disbelief
the mind protects
that which is too terrible to absorb
small pieces, fragmented
seem to play hide and seek
while the mind pretends this is a dream
from which I will awake
but each morning is the same
not even bringing with it a brief respite
each morning arrives, like the one before

Coming Out

How does one tell the world?
does one drop a hint over drinks or in between courses?
or should the topic be saved for therapy?
is this like a coming out party
that was so popular with young women back in the '50s?
or is this more like coming out of the closet
or outing as it is also known, the in thing of the '90s?
how does one come out?
does one simply say I have Alzheimer's,
no excuses, explanations needed?
or does one give a small educational lecture first?
and even more important, when does one come out,
in the beginning when it is barely noticeable
and easily covered?
or in the middle when signs can
no longer be explained away?
different doctors have different opinions
each espousing their way as most expedient
there is no one answer
and perhaps it's easier to decide
whom to come out to and whom not
one thing is certain, life will never be the same
after that courageous moment

Alike

We often thought alike
while we never finished each other's sentences
we usually were in sync
two minds paralleling each other
two minds thinking like one
how ironic, the day will come
when one mind will think for two
will I be able to think for him then?
understand what he wants?
what he needs?
it's reported Alzheimer's patients are very in tune
with caretaker's emotions
perhaps we still will be in sync

Talk to Me

Talk to me
tell me what it is like to have Alzheimer's
I want to know
I need to know
but he cannot tell me
it seems there are no words available to describe it

it is only when I lose my keys
forget where I put the bills
hunt for the millionth time for something trivial
work myself into a near panic
reproach myself for my stupidity
that he can tell me
"Now you know," he says
"Now you know"

Who Is She?

We meet at a cocktail party
she seems to know me
"How are the children she asks?"
do I know her?
who is this woman who inquires of my children?
someone obviously from the past
I anxiously scan her face searching for recognition
but find none
"The children are fine" I hear myself reply
filling in with details to buy myself some time
while searching for clues to who she might be
finding none I ask, "How are yours?"
praying desperately she has children
and while she fills me in
with all the details about her children
who, it seems, I once knew quite well
I become acutely aware of my husband's plight

Emotions

It is suddenly as if a dam burst forth and a flood of emotions are released. After the shock is absorbed there are many emotions to deal with but families report that the predominant emotion is an overwhelming sadness. Because the disease can render the patient him or her old self one moment and different the next, it leaves families questioning themselves and the diagnosis. It is not uncommon for families to get second opinions or to be at odds with each other. Members of families do not come to consensus about the diagnosis, treatment, or type of care at the same time. Each member adjusts and relates to the disease indicative of his or her own style and personality. This often adds to the sense of frustration and stress family members feel.

It is also a difficult time for the patient who has on some level an awareness of the disease. For the caregiver, it is a time of conflicting emotions: guilt over being short tempered or irritable during pre-diagnosis time period, sadness at the loss, anger at the new role and increasing responsibilities, disappointment at the way things turned out, jealously toward those more fortunate, fear of the unknown, and doubt about one's abilities to do or to even want to do the job. It is not just a time of negative emotions; it can be a time of pulling together and accessing new skills and developing inner strength. It is also a time to learn the difference between expressing or thinking emotions versus acting on them. This understanding is often the caregiver's salvation.

While there are many people who choose not to be a part of a support group, the right group can be a source of renewal and comfort. At this time, Alzheimer's disease is incurable. The current treatment plan consists of drugs to slow down the process. Since there is very little doctors can do, it is not uncommon for families to have a sense of being abandoned. Combine this with the public's fear of the disease and the resulting emotions can be acute. It is a long journey and fellow travelers make the best companions.

No Man's Land

This no man's land is a difficult place to be
in between two worlds
the one we knew
the one soon to become a reality
some days he is himself
articulate, aware, with the program
other days he is a stranger
withdrawn, closed off, aloof
it is this vacillation, back and forth, that I find so difficult

Questions

What is the disease and what is him?
a question not easily answered
a secret waiting to be unraveled
are his behaviors a result of the disease?
but he had them before
now they are just more pronounced
where does he start and where does he end?
when is he himself?
and when is he the disease?
when can I be irritated with the same
old things that have always irritated me?
and when must I be forgiving?
how do I draw the line?
the demarcation is blurred
he seems to be just more himself

Tired

I am so tired
a tiredness that goes beyond, making me wonder
if I ever will recover
how can I be so tired
this is just the beginning, even though, in truth,
it began many years before
it is a collective tiredness
made up of increased responsibilities and losses
but it just the beginning
only a year with the official diagnosis has passed
yet it seems like so many more
I don't want to see beyond today
into a tomorrow that will be worse
his dependency grows each day
I am gone, replaced by we
living a life for two
I am so tired and it is just the beginning

First Glimmer

Denial . . . they will not believe, this family of mine
what is before their very eyes
seeking solace, instead, in what has always been
I understand their reluctance to see the truth
to deal with today's reality
"Dad is fine," they assure me
as they congratulate him on how well he is doing
rejoicing in the fact the disease is moving slowly
but moving it is
am I the only one who knows that?
do they think I make these things up?
or see things that are not?
Dad is fine — listen to him speak of politics
does he not remember, they argue, each one building their
   case
each one buoying the other
yet they refuse to see how simple and uncomplicated
his life has become
how compromised he is
focusing instead on all the ways he still is Dad
until we play a simple card game
and the first glimmer of acknowledgment breaks through

Denial

Do not ask me once again if I have contacted a support group
I am not ready
why can't you see that?
why can't you respect that?
why can't you leave me to my own devices?
I will cope on my own terms
in my manner
using my intuition
after all, wasn't it
that very same intuition that
no doctor seemed to possess that brought
us to this diagnosis?
when I am ready I will go
until then let me enjoy these final days
where things are almost normal
and I can still pretend

Moments

I complain to the shrink
he does this and that
"It's the disease" he replies
I guess that must make it all right
and I want to scream at him, "That's easy for you to say,
you don't have to live with him."
in my rational moments, far and few between these days,
I know he is right
but to see my husband sitting on the couch day after day
contributing nothing while the world goes on around him
makes most of my moments less than rational

Disappointed

He is disappointed
the children did not ask, in detail, how he was or
what it is like to have this disease
at this most recent visit
I am surprised by this
I thought him not capable of such feelings
dismissed that part of him as gone for good
yet he tells me there are good days and bad
and on good days the mind works well
functioning almost as before
but on bad days it is sluggish, slow to recall
he is well aware
far more than I give him credit for
and now it is I who am disappointed
for not seeing what I should have seen

Longings

I see an elderly couple
no longer am I amused by their bond
or annoyed by their slowness
as so often was my response
new reactions have taken their place
envy . . . anger
that is what I now feel
for what they have
for what I never will have
I assumed
I believed
I bought into the golden years
I put off today
for a tomorrow
that was promised
that I was entitled to
or so I thought
I followed the rules
did all the right things
for a tomorrow that has been reneged

Bargaining

I will go back and take away each and every bad thought I
  ever had about him
live from this day forward with every irritating habit of his
  without complaining
I will go back and settle for less and not want more
I will go back and never, ever complain about his mother
  again (or at least I will try)
I will go back and be very, very good
the perfect wife
the wonderful companion
If only I could go back and do it over
I would do anything if only we could go back to yesterday

Anger

You get to do whatever you want
you get to not be held accountable
while I pick up the pieces
do the work of two
you get to focus on yourself
your right, your privilege bestowed upon you by the disease
you are accommodated
looked after, taken care of, worried about
I am exhausted, alone, weary
carrying us both
symbiotic victims
one excused
one invisible

Watch Out World

Watch out world, here I come
in my jeep ranting and raving

out of my way
I have no time

watch out world, here I come
pushing my shopping cart, barely missing you

out of my way
I have no compassion

watch out world, here I come
standing in line, watching your every move

out of my way
I have no time for you or your slowness

watch out world, here I come
a caregiver, exhausted and overwhelmed
wishing I could trade places with you
knowing I can't and hating you for it.

Thoughts

I look at my favorite picture hanging on my office wall
two beach chairs at the water's edge catching the setting sun

purchased to be a symbol, a reminder of what our future held
now I see two chairs and wonder who will sit in the other

another man?
how can I think such thoughts?

or will he sit there   . . . this man who looks like my
  husband
but is not
I hope not

how can I think such thoughts?

Backwards

I thought I was through with it
been there, done that
but now I've returned to a world I left behind years ago
I find myself going backwards
to get out of the house
once a simple event
has become a monumental undertaking
something that must be started long before departure
explained, outlined, reasons given
then the wait begins
as he moves slower than I ever thought possible
until I want to throw up my hands in despair
or simply leave, never to return

Broken

The vacuum cleaner is broken
he ran over the cord
clogged the machine with pine needles
the bottle of wine is shattered
he placed it on the ledge
forgetting all about the wine rack
the dishwasher cup is permanently stuck
he did something in mid cycle
locking it in the stuck mode
the printer is broken
the second time this month
what has he done?
God only knows
but one thing for sure, he knows it's not his fault
the angry part of me wants to yell,
"Hasn't enough been broken in our life, must you add to it?"
the empathic part wants to tell him,
like one would a child, it doesn't really matter
the tired part of me
wants to put my head down and cry
for yesterday and for the tomorrows to come

Dark Side

This disease has brought out my dark side
front and center with no place to hide
all those years of niceness
corporate wife
homeroom mom
team player at work
an image I wore comfortably and believed to be true
gone in one fell swoop
replaced now by a new image
recalcitrant
self involved
self pitying
a whole new side kept under wraps all these years
has suddenly exploded forth
with a fury all its own
where has my nice image gone
now that I need it to support my new role of caregiver?

Books

Sometimes it doesn't help me to read the books on Alzheimer's
it doesn't seem possible this is coming from me
the voracious reader
the one who scours the bookstore for the "just off the press" selections
the one who already has her own small library
dedicated solely to the topic
the one who copes by gathering all the knowledge available
but, on some level, those books, no matter how well-meaning,
no matter how inspirational they are meant to be
frighten me
leave lingering doubts and answers to questions I'm not ready to hear
and the people who tell their personal story
must be saints or darn close
not an ordinary person like myself
those people are self sacrificing
altruistic to an extreme
and even when they write of their frustration,
their anger, their tears shed
it is always noble
I don't feel noble
I feel vulnerable
frightened
overwhelmed
and very, very ordinary

Don't Get it

I just don't seem to get it
I know it's the disease that makes him behave
the way he does
but still I feel anger bubbling up inside of me
as if he could really be different if only he tried
where does this come from, this bit of irrationality?
how much more do I need to know
before I can really accept what is happening?
should I read more books?
talk to more doctors?
enroll in more support groups?
all moot questions
it is not about acceptance
I understand, I accept, there are no other options
this is about rage that at a point in our life
where the rewards were to come
we're left with what feels like punishment

Relationships

The impact of Alzheimer's is far reaching and touches the most important of all relationships down to the most trivial. It is the loss of the person with the disease that is so difficult to deal with. Losses are gradual, coming slowly and plateauing off, only to be followed by another loss. Families have the difficult task of grieving not just one loss, but many losses over an extended period of time. Part of the difficulty lies in grieving for a person who is still present in our lives, but not the same—a task defined as anticipatory grieving.

It is not just the person that families grieve but other relationships. Many people can not deal with Alzheimer's or any incurable disease, and distance themselves at a time when their friendship is most needed. Well-meaning friends offer advice but it is imperative that the caregiver listen to his or her own voice. Friends, and sometimes family who do not live with the person on a daily basis, often, inadvertently, cause the caregiver stress by telling them the person is just fine and doing very well. The only one who knows the true status is the person who is involved on a 24 hour basis. In the beginning, it is not uncommon for caregivers to collude with the illness and cover for the person, giving the appearance that all is fine. After a period of time, this behavior is no longer possible or desirable. Pretending and covering up comes with a heavy price.

The medical community often can be of very little help since there isn't much they can do. The growing awareness of the effects of caregiving have made many doctors aware of the second victim of the disease—the caregiver. A good doctor and, perhaps, a therapist can do much to relieve the caregiver's burden and to help maintain a sense of equilibrium.

The caregiver is caught walking a fine line between expressing the pain they are going through and not burdening and turning off existing friendships. Once again, a support group is where true understanding will come and is often a source of new friendships in a time of dwindling ones. It is imperative to explore and deal with one's emotions versus repressing them. In the long run it does much to ease caregiving. A primary source of one's relationships has been lost and that can bring up old unresolved issues. It is best to be guided by today's reality, as painful and unpleasant as it may be. One of the primary tasks of the caregiver is to continue to find a source of friendship to sustain them throughout the journey.

Become

His mind operates as a child's
always wanting to stop for a soda
longing for an ice cream cone
fast food a major delight
for Christmas he gave me a T-shirt,
button and fancy paper bag
exclaiming," It's the Grinch, your favorite"
and pestering me to wear it
simple pleasures are what interest him now
and form the network of his days
an uncomplicated life
early to bed, early to rise
filled in between with non-stop eating
and meaningless activity
TV or movies too difficult to follow
a quick nap serves as a reprise
politics and long-held opinions he still can espouse
conversations on feelings and dreams no longer an option
a friend, confidant, lover or husband,
roles he is no longer capable of filling
a child, a little boy, alternating between petulant
and sweet, is what he has become

Unfinished Business

We have so much unfinished business lying around
issues that were put off for tomorrow
never explored, discussed or investigated
it seemed easier at the time
life was so hectic, full of deadlines and competing priorities
tomorrow always seemed to be a better time
promised to be calmer
and surely those issues could wait
but now the expiration date is up
our time has run out
we no longer have the chance to resolve those issues
now I must live with our unfinished business
but without hope for resolution

Forgotten

We've always had a ritual
small and silly, just between the two of us
a kiss as we close the condo door
a private ending to perfect weekend in Vermont
never forgotten
even in times of rush and frenzied hurrying
until now . . . he forgot, the first time ever
I said nothing, waiting to see if he would remember
but he did not
so I told myself he was distracted
after all the roads were bad, the snow was falling
but deep down I knew we had entered a new phase
and all the times since he has not remembered
almost as if we never shared that moment

Anticipatory

I miss him
the way he used to be
the things we did together
the dreams once shared
I miss him as he sits here right next to me
I miss the future that has not yet arrived
when he will not know who I am
or where he is
but will still be present, even if only in degrees
I miss the day he will not be here
and I will have the official title of widow
not the unofficial one of married widow
anticipatory grief is what I am experiencing
part of the grieving process
allowed to occur, the actual process made shorter
but somehow it seems a waste of today
when each minute is so precious
nonetheless, I cannot stop missing him

Regression

His responses are often childish
as is his behavior
how strange it is to be a witness to this
to see him become, before my eyes, a child
without eliciting in me the feelings my children did
no maternal instinct operating here
although I feel tenderness and compassion toward his plight
I also feel irritation and discomfort
how does one become a parent to their spouse
when insect tones play havoc with the mind

Annoying

Annoying . . . I find him so annoying
I never thought it possible for anyone to be so annoying
does he have some built in radar
that keeps track of my every move?
how can we always be in the same place at the same time?
I can deal with the forgetfulness
I can overlook the same question asked over and over again
but this ability of his to track my every move
to come up behind me when I least suspect
to appear out of nowhere
to never give me a minute alone
to wait till the moment I was waiting for
on the news to interrupt
with some nonsensical question or piece of information
to be my shadow morning, noon, and night
is driving me crazy
I feel like I could jump out of my skin
he is so annoying, but who would understand
only someone who lives with him or someone
who has been through it
the others comment on how well he is doing
how good he looks
how lucky we are to still have this time together

but they're not here
prisoners in their home
playing to an audience of one
I think, some days, I will lose my mind before he loses his

Coming or Going

I look at family and friends
and wonder who will be there when this is over
who will see it through to the end
and in what capacity
I brace myself, ready for people to leave
or bow out gracefully
wondering how long they will be around
how long they will hang on
yet I know I must be careful not to send out such messages
or to drive people away
but I analyze their every word
read more into each situation
I have become hyper-vigilant
not just of the patient
but of the entire world
a shared family history of unequal roles
weighs upon my mind
friends who have come and gone through the years
cloud my outlook
the cast of characters, I think, will remain true to color
and then I wonder
am I projecting my own fears?

Support

I feel so isolated from my friends
as if we are living in different worlds
no longer speaking the same language
I sense the connection loosening
the distancing has begun
I understand and yet I don't
I would not do it to them
a friend for only the good times
what are they afraid of?
it is not catching
or is it simply they don't want to face their own mortality?
that's too easy
why should I let them off the hook
to disappear back into their safe lives
to leave me, their friend, to stand alone
when I would be there for them if the situation were reversed
but it is not
so, it is time for a support group

Leaving

The disease is taking away my husband
slowly, the rate inches along
the disease is taking away our friends
quickly, the rate progresses
it will be a slow journey for my husband
many chances to say good by
with friends it seems there will be no lingering good byes
just abrupt departures
the message couched, waiting to be deciphered
friends move away, distance themselves
build bridges to new relationships
I understand
someday I will have to do the same
but I am still here
only one of us is leaving
why can our friends not see that?

Dwindling

The phone calls have become few and far between
old friends, family and children
call less and less
conversation guarded
moratorium on certain subjects
cheerfulness the operative of the day
expediency the goal
duty the driving motive
AT&T profits dwindling
along with family, friends and children

Final Insult

I have become inured to friends leaving,
those were the fair weather ones
I am not even surprised as good friends dwindle
or shocked that certain family members call less and less
or bothered by the awkward silence, at times, of co-workers

it is a part of the disease
not written up in any medical book or journal
but there nonetheless
what shocks me is my place of work
a hospital
in the Human Resource Department of all places
a deaf ear turned to a request for a reduction of work hours
by a professional who comes in and does her work
leaving the disease at home

the bottom line
the department's own agenda more important
this is not a disease one recovers from
this is a disease that progresses each day
forcing family to enjoy what's left of today
for a tomorrow that will not be there
this reaction is the final insult

Well-Meaning

I am so tired of well-meaning friends and family
telling me how great my husband looks and acts
"He seems fine"
"Look at how healthy he is"
"He's still with the program"
"His vocabulary is as good as ever"
what is the unspoken message?
stop complaining
stop making more out of it than it is

Be happy with what you have!
I want to shout at them,
"You don't live with him 24 hours a day
you see only small pockets of our life
you see what you want to see or need to see
or perhaps you see only what you can see"
I know they mean well
do I explain the situation as it is?
lay out my frustrations and fears?
which may fall on deaf ears
or alienate them, leaving me more alone
the longer I struggle with this dilemma
the louder a voice becomes
it is time for a support group

Response

Am I depressed?
why do these doctors continue to ask me this?
what response is it that they want to such a foolish question?
"No, I am not depressed" — a socially expedient response
returning the focus to the patient
"Yes, I am depressed" — an honest response
forcing them to now listen to a litany of caregiver's complaints
what is it I am to answer?
who would not be depressed?
only a person devoid of emotions and not in touch with reality
I am not devoid of emotions nor am I out of touch with reality
but perhaps that is what I must become in order to survive
perhaps I need to adhere to the standard medical model
buoying up the statistics on depression in caregivers
but I am not depressed, as much as I am overwhelmed
I can still cope and find my way through the maze
juggle home and work
why can't doctors forget the clinical jargon and
let the caregiver use her own descriptor
why is it the course of this disease is unique for each patient
but the response of the caregiver
must fit a prescribed medical mode?

Advice

"Just take him home and love him."
that's how I know my visit with the neurologist
is coming to an end
it's his sage advice dispensed at the close of each visit
but what does it mean?
there is no hope
there is nothing more I can do
and how does it apply how to me?
am I to be a courtesan
or simply just the devoted wife?
does it imply I am not seeing the big picture
grasping the situation in its entirety?
or is it simply reality wrapped in nice words?
this is a terrible thing that should happen to no one

Equal Opportunity

We are not to judge the patient's behavior
no matter how bizarre
no matter how obstructive it has become
no matter how threatening it seems
we, the caregivers, are to accept it as part of the disease
neither intentional nor personal
to understand the driving force behind it
to change our reaction to it
that's what the books say
that's what the experts say
that's what those who have gone before say
who am I to argue with collective wisdom
dispute well meaning experts
or risk them taking umbrage?
no longer will I judge
from this moment on I will accept and understand
what I have no control over
and work, instead, on changing my reactions
not only to him, the patient
but for me the caregiver
this must be an equal opportunity change

Accommodation

I must make accommodations, the doctor tells me
this wise man who is guiding me through this nightmare
this medical man who is partnering with me
as I become the voice of the patient,
the reporter of the status quo
this man, compassionate and kind
who has not hidden behind a medical mask
of indifference or professionalism
as so often happens

he assures me I can say anything I want to him
but I wonder if it is true
afraid to test the limits, push the envelope
my husband is leaving me day by day
my friends are slowly disappearing
I dare not lose him, too
in an illness where the medical profession
sends you home to die

so I agree with him when he says I must not be so honest
it serves no purpose for my husband at this point
I must learn to accommodate
I understand
but when he tells me to make his life wonderful,

to love and cherish him
I want to yell,
I want to shout
there are two people here in this equation
why have you not noticed?

Micromanagement

I understand now what the neurologist is saying
with new clarity
a long time coming
he says I want to micromanage the disease
not in an insulting manner, but as matter of fact
before I heard it as not being compliant
not doing right by the patient
now I understand
this style of mine that has always worked
won't work with this disease
I can micromanage from A to Z
orchestrate our lives
tie up financial loose ends
oversee advanced directives
but I can not micromanage this disease
it will follow its own course
micromanaging us along the way

Hidden

Friends comment on how well I am doing
on my ability to handle whatever comes my way
I see admiration in their faces
mixed with compassion
or perhaps it's simply relief it's not them
people tell me I will make it through
be just fine one day
can they tell me when that day will be?
have they forgotten this journey is about years
or are they just grateful to not be traveling down this road?
the therapist I am seeing throws out a question
for me to ponder
"do you not think they respect you?"
is he waiting for an answer or is the question rhetorical?
is it his way of telling me he respects me?
or is he just relieved his patient is holding it together?
would they all be so full of admiration
so sure I'll make it through
or so quick to bestow me with their respect
if they knew the angry thoughts I keep hidden
safe within myself?

Weekend Away

We went away this weekend
the two of us and my good friend
and she spent the weekend telling me
how great he was doing
how wonderful he looked

and I wondered all weekend
does she not see that he does not understand the dinner bill?
that he can no longer figure out a simple tip?
did she not see how confused
he became over simple matters?
or the increasing errors he made?
was she not aware of the constant reassurances he needed
or of the tentativeness of his manner?
did she not question why I drove the entire trip
laced up his snowshoes
and spent a good part of the weekend
searching for misplaced items?

to the public Alzheimer's is the final stages
the stuff in between doesn't fit the stereotype
only the caregiver knows the seamless appearance of life
is well orchestrated by one person functioning for two

The New Me

My friends all comment on how patient I am
what a nice job I'm doing
strangers, once they know, marvel that I'm still smiling
taking it all so well
acquaintances think it noble I speak about the disease
and share my insights with others

co-workers congratulate me that I can still do my job
my family thinks I'm handling it all so well
I have obtained a new level of maturity
people look at me with awe
and with new respect
I feel like any day I will be canonized
or, at the very least, beatified
what they don't see
even though I share it with them
they seem unwilling to hear
is that I am tired and cranky many a day
that horrendous, horrible thoughts run through my head

nor do they pick up on my tense body language
irritating remarks I make fall on deaf ears
it is more comfortable to canonize me
it is more convenient to beatify me
make me something special

almost more than human
for if I were human
instead of this special person they have turned me into
then, they too could be caught
in the devastation of this disease

Why

Why do they say those things to me?
"You don't want to know"
"What lies ahead is better left unknown"
the survivors of this ordeal
the ones who have gone before
why do they look at me with knowing eyes
seeing what I can not
seeing what I eventually will see
what is it they know that I must know?
what is it they have lived through,
and will I, too, live through?
I want to ask them those questions but I am frozen in fear
of what their answers will be
I do not want to know
but I need to know to prepare myself
so I teeter back and forth
poised to ask, receptive to hear
settling last minute on not asking what needs to be asked
preferring silence
hoping downcast eyes will shield me from the truth
hide my cowardice
not knowing if they are ally or adversary
not knowing if I want to know or not

Support Group

It seems they all start with good intentions
these ladies in my support group
each declaring undying devotion
no husband of theirs to ever go into a nursing home
and I watch with fascination their loyalty
wondering where mine is as they declare
they will keep their husbands at home
bring in outside help
turn the family room into a bedroom
the house into a fortress
good intentions abound
sincere and from the heart
but one by one as the disease progresses
the good intentions break down
thoughts turn to possibilities of nursing homes
as physical demands increase
the hold of promises loosen as fatigue sets in
the resolve behind the good intentions wavers
as one by one these ladies in my support group
grow more weary with each passing day

Holidays

Loss is never felt as poignantly as it is during the holidays or special days that mark an anniversary or milestone. The whole world seems to be joyous and the sense of one's pain can seem even more acute and isolating. Many caregivers try to hold onto the past and recreate a holiday as it always has been. This places an additional burden on them. It is best to acknowledge that things have changed and so has the celebration. Often what lies behind the fear is the dread of the future and the unknown.

This can be a good time, if one is the main keeper of the holiday, to turn it over to someone else and take advantage of being a guest. There isn't a caregiver in the world who wouldn't benefit from being a guest. In fact, that may be the best gift family or friends can offer.

Because things are different doesn't mean that special times can't be enjoyed. One of the lessons of the disease seems to be about the ability to live in the moment. Families have an opportunity to learn and practice this on a daily basis.

Memories

I am the keeper of the holidays and special anniversaries
the one in charge of orchestrating events
preserving family traditions
blending in changing families and new ways
it's a role not uncommon to women
in which we carry most of the responsibility
sometimes begrudgingly, but mostly with understanding
for with it come the memories
well worth the work
well worth the sacrifices
memories to be shared in years to come
with family members not yet born
to validate and honor all that has gone before
to soften growing older
now I find I am to be keeper of the memories, too

Spring

Spring has arrived after a long winter of endless tests
doctors' appointments
hopes raised
hopes dashed
bringing with it, as always, the promise of new beginnings
but not for us
endings are all I can see
and paramount in my mind are the questions
no one can seem to answer,
is this the last spring the way we are?

Trip

Four months, almost to day of the dreaded diagnosis,
we depart for a trip to Italy
Italian landscape passes before my eyes, a mere blur
Venice is rainy, matching my spirit
the countryside warm and friendly, beckoning
but I stay locked in my cocoon of shock
this long awaited trip was to be a celebration
now it is a respite
a chance to gain some equilibrium
before the next onslaught
why did we put it off so long?
how were we to know
what else have we put off for a tomorrow that will not come?

Lesson from Venice

I fell in love with Venice
a city in decay
a parallel not lost on me
it was magical
in a world now devoid of magic
the rain a slow and steady drizzle
never ending
matching the progress of the disease
in spite of it all
I fell in love with Venice
seeing beyond the decay
the unrelenting rain
to a magic that remained in spite of all the odds

Holidays

It's holiday time again but this year it's different,
very different
this year we are well aware
there's a third party celebrating with us
I want to grab the proverbial Thanksgiving wishbone
and wish this not true
do I hang a stocking for this intruder
who has become a member of our family?
set another place at the Christmas table?
ask him to give the New Year's toast?
instead I wonder
what will we be thankful for next Thanksgiving?
will we be able to be together next Christmas,
this family so separated by miles?
what will the New Year bring?
but I dare not ask
I am the preserver of the holidays, the family traditions
and this year's holiday season is bittersweet
that to worry about next year would rob of us this season
so I keep my thoughts to myself,
sharing them with no one
wanting to preserve what we still have left
wanting to pretend it's not happening

wanting this holiday season to be perfect
and wondering if this is the last holiday season
as the family we have been

Christmas This Year

Christmas this year will be the same, outwardly
everyone will be jolly
working hard to please and be congenial
manners up to par
old grievances put aside
sibling rivalries given the day off
trying hard to be that Hallmark Christmas family
if just for only one day
another perfect Christmas once again the goal
but inwardly things will be different
for this year "perfect" has taken on a new meaning

Perfect

It is holiday time again
the season of good cheer
the time to let bygones be gone
a time of forgiveness
and coming together
to remember good friends and good times
a picture perfect season
full of picture perfect people

is that why we've been forgotten
removed from this year's party list
now that we no longer fit that perfect picture
we serve as a reminder
no one is safe
no one immune to life's tragedies

that there is no forgiveness with this disease is tragic
that there is no forgiveness with friends is heartbreaking
after all, it is only last year we were picture perfect, too
and on everyone's list

Wonderful

Life's not so wonderful this year
the Christmas cards are coming in
one by one
everyone's life seems to be wonderful this year
new grandchildren
retirements to exotic spots
trips around the world
sometimes I wonder are we the only ones
whose life is falling apart?
what should I write on cards?
no grandchildren on the horizon
retirement no longer an option
trips around the world not on our agenda
life's not so wonderful this year

365 Days Ago

How different this holiday season is than last
when the possibility of brain tumor,
not too large nor malignant, hung over us
when a diagnosis of depression
would have been a welcome event
when surely there was nothing really wrong
and if there were, certainly there was a cure
just 365 days ago, the world as we knew it
was safe and secure
now the world looms, uncertain and unwelcoming

Black

My Christmas packing for the long awaited visit is complete
black velvet dress
black velvet pants and top
black sweater
black knit pants
black long skirt
black tights and shoes
is this unconscious behavior on my part?
does it reflect depression?
am I trying out widowhood?
or is black simply in this season?
the color de rigueur

Relinquish

There's ice in Atlanta, an almost unheard of event
but nothing surprises me anymore
it seems we're not getting out
my daughter tearful on the other end of the phone
well aware the clock is ticking for her father
has planned the perfect Christmas
one to be remembered for Christmases to come
my son, 2,000 miles away, paralyzed by indecision
my parents, too elderly to drive, but too stubborn to listen
unreachable on the road somewhere
so I rise to the occasion, once again
without even realizing it
taking charge
checking airlines for alternatives
remaining cheerful and optimistic
careful to keep the family spirits up
salvage the holiday
a parallel to my role with the disease
only this time the toll is greater
I can not do it all
shoulder the disappointments
weather the storm
keep everyone going

my own pain so great
my weariness so deep
I must relinquish the role
it's time to become a recipient

Lost Him

I lost him in the Atlanta Airport
momentarily, but it seemed like a lifetime
he said he had to go to the bathroom
and I, involved, in all the details of changing planes
paid little attention
but as minutes passed a quiet fear came over me
along with the knowledge I did not know
what he was wearing
that I should have been more alert
he is now my responsibility, totally
this is all new to me
watching over a grown man who is my husband
who once watched over me
he returned twenty minutes later
like a young boy, looking sheepish but relieved
and we both agreed how confusing the
Atlanta Airport could be
how much a hassle travel had become
saving face another chore added
to the caregiver's job description

Talk

They talk about the millennium
and what it will bring
they make plans for the future
that for them will come
how can I talk about something so far away
when I don't even know about tomorrow?
how can I be excited about new promises
when I have all I can do to deal with today's realities?
they see their future as bright
full of new beginnings
I see my future as bleak
full of endings
sometimes I wonder how we can be so far apart
how our worlds can be so disparate?

Unrelenting

I'm filling out my pocket calendar for the new year
who do I put in case of emergency?
this disease so cruel, so unrelenting
comes home to hit you at every bend in the road
and if that's not enough, when you least expect it
there is no respite
no time to forget
it won't let you
it scatters reminders throughout your life
that it is here
it is in control
things are different
never to be the same
nothing ever to be taken for granted again

Impact

The cost of the financial toll on the healthcare system has been well documented over the years. The real devastation lies in the impact on the caregiver and the families of people suffering from Alzheimer's. Dollars and cents can be measured but the emotional cost to families can not. It is not uncommon, especially among the elderly caregivers, for a caregiver to become ill themselves or die from the stresses of what has been termed "the 36 hour day."

The caregiver is the one who has been living with the knowledge, consciously or unconsciously, of the disease for the *longest time. This in itself extracts a high price.* As caregivers struggle to make sense, to cope, to hold their head above water, to keep it all together, to pick up new responsibilities, it is no wonder that an already taxed system would go on overload. It is a role for whom very few are prepared, very few want, and it comes with no job description, vacation, or benefits. Add to that list, no public recognition, and the fact that almost always the job and majority of the responsibility falls to one person who is the "designated" caregiver in a family.

Many factors can complicate matters: previous relationships, unfinished business, old family roles. It is beneficial to learn as much about the disease as possible in order to understand the dynamics and the requisite skills. For many women, who have had years of mothering or caregiving, there seems to be no respite. It is imperative that caregivers find a way to make time for themselves. Good decisions are never made in an exhausted state and the world can look much different with a good night's sleep. Caregiving requires a sharing of the responsibility and it usually is up to the caregiver to ask for what he or she needs, not wait for others to figure it out. Becoming clear about one's priorities and paying attention to one's own needs, benefit not just the caregiver but the patient.

Specimen

I am tired of being poked and prodded mentally
stared at
observed
evaluated
my words
my thoughts no longer belong to me
now they have become part of the medical record
part of the disease
does she understand?
can she cope?
how much can she absorb?
is she moving through the steps?
is she marching to the tune?
I want to scream, "I am not the patient"
but I have become the patient
I am the eyes, voice, and mind
so I must be observed and evaluated

Catastrophize

It is hard not to catastrophize
when I go into his bathroom and find
everything in disarray
the bottom of the picture frame lying on the floor
an unflushed toilet covered with spots of dried urine
the sink full of toothpaste
and the tub with a ring around it that will take hours to clean
the vacuum cleaner makes a loud humming noise
the electric broom no longer picks up
the soap cup is broken in the dishwasher
the microwave and coffee pot
look like they haven't been cleaned in months
yet it was only last weekend I did both
the dryer is on borrowed time
both cars have passed 100,000 miles
various rooms in the house are in dire need of paint
the driveway is breaking up with each winter storm
it's hard not to catastrophize when I bear the burden alone

I Wish

I am so bone weary tired
my mind is overwhelmed and not one more detail can it hold
my body aches from overwork, without respite
a full nights unbroken sleep no longer an option
my life unencumbered a thing of the past
I wish there were someone to take care of me
sometimes I even wish I were the patient
and not the caregiver

Shadowing

I can put up with a lot
look the other way
be responsible for both my life and his
but what I can not do is deal with his shadowing
I am never alone
he always finds a reason to be in the room I am
to rummage through the drawers
looking for God knows what
to check out some inconsequential piece of information
and if I take a bath it is not long before I hear him
in the closet
changing his clothes or in search of the elusive something
a nap on a weekend is an event for two
a walk or an errand is something one does not do alone
he is with me at every turn I take
my only peace is when he falls asleep watching TV
but, with the sensitivity of a dog, he awakens
if I try to steal out of the room

Straighten Up

I want to straighten up everything in sight
not just the kitchen
of which he has made another colossal mess
or his den which looks like a war zone
or the car littered with coffee cups and fast food wrappers
I want to straighten up the details of our life that have
   suddenly been left to me
as he goes about making these messes . . . oblivious to it all
finances in a state of disarray
wills to be finalized
stock options and future plans lying without direction
but I am in my own state of chaos
as messy as the kitchen, den, and car

Understanding

I understand now why widows talk so much
my mother-in-law, in particular,
from whom I often wish to hide
although I am not a widow in the technical sense
I am a widow of a different kind
a married widow
living with a man
sharing a life together
bereft of communication on a deeper level
not aware till now of
how much I talk in social situations
more than my share
bordering on domination
not to mention bad manners and boorishness
the words flow out
uncensored, manic at times
wishing to be heard
wishing to be acknowledged
I, who go to work each day and converse
but it is not the same
I miss the intimacies
the easy conversation, unguarded
the sharing on a deeper level that comes with a husband

I am tired of the basics that rule our life
and our conversations
I yearn for real communication
a connection that words supply
a bridge to the soul
instead I must make do with trivialities
fearing the day when even that will be gone

Destined

How could this happen to me?
I do not have what it takes to be a caregiver
needing to be involved in others' lives
always on the alert for someone to take care of
self sacrificing
I've been there, done that
years of mothering
playing the corporate wife
living alone, putting my career on the back burner
to advance his

supporting the family through numerous downsizings
helping launch our son after his divorcee
changing plans for the widowed mother-in-law
I've paid my dues
made the sacrifices
done what was expected and then some
put my life on hold

this was to be a time for me
to discover who I am
who I want to be
a time to be selfish
am I destined to be in service all my life?

Repertoire

There are so many roles I play in this new life of mine
I can hardly keep count as I
go in and out of them in response to him
some I am well prepared for, others brand new
roles I never thought I would play
I have become accustomed to
but the role of warden, the role of bad guy
is one I like the least
I find myself locked in power struggles
feeling one moment his pain
understanding how his life is being taken away
but in the next moment seeing clearly
he is not capable of doing certain things
and the risk far surpasses personal needs
there is no way for both to win
there are no concessions to be made
this is purely black and white
and I have become the enemy

Promise

Years ago I lay on the surgeon's table,
breath held tightly in,
body motionless as I awaited the pathologist's report
would the breast biopsy be malignant or benign?
the odds were not in my favor
I reviewed my life to date
one soon to leave for college, one still in high school
years of sacrifices still to be made
but if I was OK, I vowed
I would find some time for just me
the gods of fate gave me another chance
in gratitude, I promised
this would be a lesson remembered
but life returned to normal and a promise soon forgotten
two years ago I lay in the pre-op room
waiting for the anesthesiologist
wondering if the tumors were benign
knowing, either way, I would awake, without my ovaries
once again I reviewed my life
children both out of college and on their own
now my life consisted of an unemployed husband
and elderly parents with pressing needs

that shaped my days
once again I made the promise, if I were all right
I would find some time for me
how was I to know?

Coping

How does one cope? There is no answer because it is a highly individual response. The best advice I can give from my own experience is to stay true to one's feelings, go with your intuition, and accept yourself as less than perfect and doing the best job possible at that moment and time.

Just as the caregiver's coping style is a reflection of their uniqueness so is the patient's adjustment and coping to the disease a reflection of their uniqueness. Individual differences, idiosyncrasies, and preferences must be taken into account. Being judgmental, bitter, and angry, while understandable, are not helpful skills.

It is helpful to remember that each behavior has a meaning and is a form of communication. Familiarize yourself with the terms cueing, shadowing, distancing and other Alzheimer jargon. Be open to new ways of being, and learn from those who have gone before you; they are your best teachers and guides. Changes must come from the caregiver as the patient is not capable of changing his or her behavior.

It is said that no caregiver makes the journey unchanged. I believe this to be true. Already I have seen changes in myself. I have learned to not ask why, or dwell on only ifs. I simply ask for the courage and strength needed for the journey, and to not become bitter or cynical. I also hope for a cure; if not now, then for future generations. And my thoughts are with all the families dealing with this devastating disease.

Speaks

She speaks to me with softness in her voice
this young psychologist I have been referred to
regarding research on caregivers
I feel an instant connection,
visceral in nature coming through the phone
she is someone who goes beyond the research data
we talk of adaptive styles
the influence of genetics versus learned behavior
she says it is a different kind of loss
than from death or divorce
nothing I haven't heard already
but from her I hear it differently
she comments on how difficult it must be
and I agree, with short stories to punctuate the point
careful not to burden her
she is not the first to reach out in kindness
but she is the first to evoke tears
thank God for the privacy of the phone
this woman I never met
has made a small hole in my protective armor
and in my need to hold it all together

Good Intentions

I will not be cowed by this disease
I will not be overcome or destroyed
nor will I partner with it in its destruction
good intentions, that's what I have
but are they enough to see me
through the vicissitudes that lie ahead?
what does it take to ensure one's safety at the other end?
optimism mixed with reality
supportive friends and family
unlimited resources
strong, unerring faith
determination and resilience
I wish there were a set formula to follow
but like the disease, each person is unique
each person left to follow a singular path

Changes

This place of work where I had
begun the countdown
distanced myself emotionally
continued to get the job done
but with less wear and tear
erected new boundaries
counted my days as numbered
has suddenly changed to become an oasis
a refuge from home and its inherent problems
a keeper of my sanity
a place where I need to be, want to be
my structure in this new world without structure
my life is changing in all arenas

Translation

It is one thing to read about Alzheimer's
in literature and books
it's quite another to experience it first hand
he can no longer sequence
a simple task that requires two steps,
ensures one will remain unfinished
how many times in the past
have I been annoyed with him over this
his failure to follow through
even after the diagnosis,
I couldn't quite believe it, didn't quite get it
he couldn't sequence
I couldn't make the translation
but today I saw it, as if for the first time
my frustration and anger on hold
today I made the translation

Cueing

Cueing . . . it's what I've instinctively done all along
do you have your wallet?
did you remember to take your pills?
have you written down the instructions?
would you like to go to bed?
some would call it nagging
some would argue women have
used it for years and men are immune
but the Alzheimer's literature regards it as the holy grail
almost like a mantra enabling one to get through the day
what is the big deal I would ask myself
each time I came across the word
which was very often
this is second nature, nothing new
but today I cued in the true sense of the definition
today I had to remind him to take a bath

Whiny

I can hear myself
there is a whiny quality about me
not in the voice but in the way I speak about things
my spirit is diminished
perhaps to parallel his diminished mind
there is nothing I can do to stop his downward spiral
but I can and must stop mine

Coping

Coping is unique to each individual
almost like a signature
I, the caregiver, cope by writing
he, the patient, copes by eating
food has become his lifeline, his coping mechanism
he is never without it
a cup of coffee or a drink in his hand
the requisite yogurt
full of antioxidants sure to fight off the disease
a bowl of ice cream late at night
during the day numerous time-outs for a snack
and in the wake
are all the telltale dishes and candy wrappers

food, once important, has now become an obsession
two lunches have become commonplace
having forgotten that he had the first
his appetite grown ravenous
each outing punctuated by fast food stops
each evening's entertainment
marked by the opening and shutting of the refrigerator door
no bedtime complete without the requisite nightcap
even when he's aroused from a deep sleep on the couch
food has become his lifeline

all he seems to care about
all that holds his interest
other aspects of his life forgotten
but not food, it remains his sole pleasure
his lifeline, his means of coping

Two Faced

I speak with the doctor
setting the tone
asking for the truth
no embellishments needed
just the facts . . . imperative that I understand
imperative that I know the truth
how else can I deal?
I speak with my husband
letting him set the tone
celebrating that there are twenty
current drugs in the pipeline
agreeing that a cure is just around the corner
remarking on how well
his self designed regiment to beat the odds is doing
what other choices do I have?
who am I to take away his hope?
it's all he has left
and soon enough the disease will take that

I Want to Shout

He should not drive
but he will not hear of this

who has he hit recently?
has he run over anyone since the diagnosis?
his record remains unblemished

"For how long?" I want to shout
but he would not hear
so slowly I take over the driving
easing myself into the role of chauffeur

He wants to continue to do the bills
after all he has always done them
a director of finance in another time and place
financial acumen once his thing
not gone . . . just needing more time

"But what about the mounting errors and the final notices?"
I want to shout
but what does he care
so I hire an accountant
and become a diplomat when he takes the credit

He wants to ski
even after his doctor has said it's a risk

against all odds he wants to ski
believing himself immune to the mountain's whims
after all he's skied for years
and what is the purpose of owning a ski home?

"I give up" I want to shout, tired of being the bad guy
but his mind is made up
until I give a performance worthy of an Oscar
converting him to snowshoeing
once I would have called this game playing
outright manipulation
downright deviousness
now I call it coping
simply getting through the day
a survival mechanism
shame and guilt no longer a part of my vocabulary
or emotional repertoire

Symbiosis

This disease so full of subtle tricks and turns
one day he is his former self
I start to believe it is only a bad dream
from which I have finally awakened
the next day he clearly is not
the man I've known all these years
and the nightmare has returned
slowly and insidiously he moves in and out
changes coming so slowly that they are hard to notice
plateauing until gradually they are accepted
as part of his repertoire
and the caregiver follows suit in order to survive
and make it through
adapting and accommodating in rhythm with the disease
partnering and plateauing in sync
two lives made symbiotic

Shades of Gray

I ask him to do something simple
so very basic
just to help me out
I can not do it all
but then I wonder why I asked at all
everything is monumental
bordering on insurmountable
and I feel the anger rise
why can't he do it?
why can't you help, just once?
why must he be this way?
why is this happening to us?
how can I ask these questions
for which I already know the answer
I who pride myself on seeing the truth
dealing with reality
not seeing denial as a viable option
I am learning it is not that simple
this disease does not deal in black and white
but instead in shades of gray
more than I ever new existed

Distancing

Distancing   . . . do we even know we're doing it?
is there a definition for this phenomenon
or is it only found in clinical textbooks?
I have started to pull away
in small measures to protect myself
not even a conscious gesture on my part
I have become slightly removed
not as vested in the future
I see myself less as a couple, more alone
family talks to me as if he were not there
not meaning to be unkind
once again not conscious
but acutely aware of the differences
he has become diminished in our eyes
are we acting in reaction to him or to our own needs?

Morning Coffee

My morning ritual of a cup of coffee
has taken on new meaning
each morning over the years
he has brought me a cup, faithfully
but now I find I hold my breath
waiting to hear his footsteps on the stairs
and if he is late, even only a matter of minutes,
I fear he has forgotten
I fear he has moved into the next stage
but he appears, so far, and I give thanks
for another day allotted
and so my days have become dependent upon a cup of coffee
a signal that, for now, things are status quo

Zack

Zack, the beloved family dog
my husband's companion through it all
best buddy to share walks and snacks with
couch potatoes together on the sofa
is dying
diagnosed before my husband
companions in the same journey
one has amyloids to the brain
the other to the kidneys
has amazed all the doctors
beaten the odds of the time frame given
and taught us to believe in hope
but most important, to not spend the days in countdown

Two Worlds

I reside in two worlds
the outer world that sees me as
coping beautifully
efficient
patient
kind and caring
and the inner world
where I see me as
pushed beyond my limits
angry
tired
annoyed and resentful
two worlds that never spill over into each other
if I try to share my inner world I am met with
it's OK
you're just tired
things will get better
and if I try to see myself as others see me I am met with
my belief that I am fraudulent
capable of fooling the world
incapable of seeing what others see
somewhere between these two worlds is the real me
but I can't seem to find a balance

instead I bounce back and forth
between two worlds of black and white
while struggling with a disease that knows only grays

What Does it Mean?

"Create your own world . . . you must begin now"
what does that mean?
I've heard it again from yet another doctor
I can add him to the scores of well meaning friends,
family and strangers
how do I create my own world when I am living life for two?
where is there time when I spend my days picking up after him
keeping track of bills and appointments?
arranging his days so his life flows without stress
my life is dictated by his schedule, by his regime,
by the confines of this disease
and who will look after him while I am out creating my own life?
is there some switch out there that will let me
turn my life on and off?
and what is the definition of your own world?
a brief respite
a movie
dinner out with the girls
or does it encompass more?
and if so, how can I create my own world when
the world I am trapped in will go on for many more years?
and the bigger question that begs to be asked
when this is all over will there be anything left of me?

Going Away

I am going away on a business trip
my first since the diagnosis
I am going away without him
something I've rarely down in all the years of marriage
this time it is different
I can't wait
I feel like a prisoner who has escaped
or, at very least, been given a parole

Real Message

I am going away on a business trip and
the first thing I am asked by
family and friends is
"What about Don?"
I return from the business trip and
the first thing I am asked by
family and friends is
"How is Don?"
I understand their concern but what ever happened to
start your own life
take care of yourself
be good to yourself
I know the question voices their concern about our situation
a legitimate one
but inherent too is the unspoken message
that negates all their well meaning advise
and leaves me to wonder what is the real message

One Year

It has been a year since the diagnosis
much of which has been lived in shock
and frantic activity revolving around
obtaining second opinions
getting finances in order
telling family and friends
it has been a year spent
alternately grieving losses and fearing the future
now on the anniversary of this ominous date
it is time to slow down and make peace with this disease
another year cannot be sacrificed in futility
the present needs to be committed to and enjoyed
so the past can be something to borrow from
when the future arrives

Fellow Journeyers

I see them as we stop in the piazza to have a drink
another family on vacation
a couple and their severely handicapped child
in a wheelchair
and I wonder what the vacation is like for them
I see them at the beach club we belong to
a mother alone with her mentally challenged grown son
and I wonder where the father went
and how the mother copes all by herself
I see them at the mall
a young couple with their children
one of whom has Down's syndrome
and I wonder if they ever ask why
and how they deal with their fate
I have seen them over the years
but before I dismissed them
with empathy for their plight
with thanks it was not mine
now I no longer want to dismiss them,
but ask instead,
are you bitter?
what is your life like?
how does one adjust, make peace?

do you believe God never gives you
more than you can handle?
is it truly a blessing in disguise?
but I don't ask
it would be presumptuous of me
instead I watch them, study them for clues
and wonder why fate choose them
knowing, now, we are fellow travelers
on an unplanned journey

RESOURCES

Alzheimer's Association
919 North Michigan Ave., Suite 1000
Chicago, IL 60611-1676
1 800 272-3900

Alzheimer's Disease Education & Referral Center
P.O. Box 8250, Silver Springs MD 20907-8250
1 800 438-4380

These organizations provide literature, support and referral resources to families and caregivers.

SUGGESTED READINGS

Brandt, Avrene, Ph.D., 1997. Caregiver's Reprieve: A Guide to Emotional Survival When You're Caring for Someone You Love. San Luis Obispo, California: Impact Publishers.

Coughlan Patricia, 1993. Facing Alzheimer's: Family Caregiver's Speak. New York: Ballantine Books.

Gruetzner, Howard, 1992. Alzheimer's: A Caregiver's Guide And Source Book. New York: John Wiley And Sons, Inc.

Grubbs, William, 1997. In Sickness and Health: Caring for a Loved One with Alzheimer's. Forest Knolls, California: Elder Books.

Hodgson, Harriet, 1995. Alzheimer's, Finding The Words: A Communication Guide for Those Who Care. Minneapolis, Minnesota: Chronimed.

Erin Tierney & Douglas H. Kramp, 1998. Living with the End in Mind. New York: Three Rivers Press.

Mace, Nancy, M.A. and Peter V. Rabins, MD, M.P.H. 1981. The 36 Hour Day. New York: Time Warner.

Manning, Doug, 1985. When Love Gets Tough: The Nursing Home Dilemma. San Francisco, California: Harper San Francisco.

McGowin, Diana Friel, 1993. Living In The Labyrinth: A Personal Journey Through The Maze of Alzheimer's. New York: Delta.

Nelson James Lindemann and Hilde Lindemann Nelson, 1996. Alzheimer's: Answers To Hard Questions for Families. New York: Doubleday.

ABOUT THE AUTHOR

Susan Miller is a family caregiver, lecturer and workshop presenter on various facets of Alzheimer's for family and professional caregivers, an Alzheimer's support group facilitator, and group member. She holds an MS in counseling and has spent the last ten years in the healthcare field.

Currently she is working on the second book of the *Unplanned Journey* trilogy — *Adapting To The Terrain*. She is available through Kaleidoscope Kare for the following:

WORKSHOPS / LECTURES

Up Close & Personal: A Caregiver's Story
Looking Through The Kaleidoscope of Professional Caregiving
Understanding Family Dynamics
The Process of Change And Letting Go
The Resilience Factor In Caregiving
New Beginnings
Poetry Readings/Discussions from Unplanned Journey

To contact Susan for more information about her workshops or lectures, or to place an order for a book, call (203) 762-5713.

ORDER FORM

Unplanned Journey: Understanding the Itinerary

Number of Copies:_____@ $9.95 .... _____

Sales tax 6%.. _____
(Conneticut residents only)

Shipping & handling .... _____
(first book $3, additional books $1)

        TOTAL .... _____

Name:_____

Address:_____

City:_____ State:_____ Zip_____

Please photocopy and complete this form, then send to:

Kaleidoscope Kare
110 Pheasant Run Road
Wilton, CT 06897